W9-ALX-133

CUT
and
COLOR
Flannel Board Stories

BOOK TWO
Learning Concepts

by Karen G. Noel

- *No drawing*
- *No tracing*

Publishers
T. S. Denison and Co., Inc.
Minneapolis, Minnesota

T. S. DENISON & COMPANY, INC.

No part of this publication may be reproduced or transmitted by any means, mechanical or electronic, including photocopy, recording, or stored in any information storage or retrieval system without permission from the publisher. Reproducible pages may be duplicated by the classroom teacher for use in the classroom, but not for commercial sale. Reproduction for an entire school or school system is strictly prohibited.

Standard Book Number: 513-01788-7
Copyright © 1985 by T. S. Denison & Co., Inc.
Minneapolis, Minnesota 55431

CONTENTS

To Meghan Downey Rob

The Author

Karen G. Noel, instructor of Early Childhood Education at MiraCosta College, Oceanside, California, is also the supervising teacher at the lab school there. She has given workshops on pre-reading and language development for parents, students and teachers.

Karen is a portrait painter and has combined her interests in art with her experience in education to produce this book.

Introduction

This is a book for preschool and kindergarten teachers. It is for the new teacher who would like to use the flannel board, and it is for the experienced teacher who would like to add to his/her collection of flannel board materials.

This book is unusual in the sense that it is not meant to be kept as a book, but will be cut and organized into actual flannel board stories. No drawing or tracing is required. The illustrations are clear and appropriately sized to be used with both large and small groups of children. The paper is of a quality and weight that will hold up with use.

The interests and needs of young children are the themes of the stories and rhymes, and they are written to encourage thought, conversation and participation. Additional ideas for activities are listed after most stories.

It is said that a picture is worth a thousand words. Use of the flannel board enables a child to experience both auditory and visual messages, allowing the teacher to communicate more fully.

The Flannel Board

The flannel board is a popular and successful teaching aid for the classroom.
It has many advantages:
- it encourages children to participate
- it enables the teacher to present various concepts
- it develops vocabulary and verbal skills
- it develops listening skills
- it holds attention and stimulates interest
- it increases the enjoyment of story telling
- it is easy to make (an average size is 18" x 24"; cover the board with a neutral color of flannel or felt material, or cover one side with a light color and the other with a dark color)
- it is easy to store
- it is convenient and simple to use with a little practice

Certain techniques will insure your success with the flannel board:
- don't crowd the board (as you add pieces, take others off)
- organize the pieces ahead of time so the story will go smoothly
- use left-to-right sequence in placing pieces on the board
- your voice is important—it should be heard by all children and modulated to hold interest
- the pieces should be brightly colored and easily identified
- remember to tilt the board so the pieces will adhere
- encourage as much participation as possible

Materials

- transparent tape
- package of sandpaper (can be purchased at hardware or grocery store)
- scissors
- rubber cement or white glue
- magic markers, crayons or colored pencils
- flannel board

Directions

Choose the particular story that you want to use and follow this procedure:
- make sure you have all the pieces (drawings) needed for the story—the text of each story has a circled number that indicates the number of pieces for that story
- cut the page(s) out of the book
- color each piece with bright colors (specific colors are indicated for some)
- finish cutting out each piece
- number each piece (on the back) to indicate the sequence of use in the story
- glue a piece of sandpaper on the back of each drawing (this will make it stick to the flannel board)
- cut out the correct text for the story or rhyme
- keep all the story pieces in a manila folder and glue the story text on the front of the folder
- make a folder for each story or rhyme and keep them in a file box

Raindrops

Raindrops, raindrops, where did they fall?   *(put up piece for cloud with raindrops)*

They fell on a red bug, but that's not all.   *(put up bug)*

Raindrops, raindrops, where did they fall?
They fell on a green frog, but that's not all.   *(put up frog)*

Raindrops, raindrops, where did they fall?
They fell on a purple flower, but that's not all.   *(put up flower)*

Raindrops, raindrops, where did they fall?
They fell on a orange cat, but that's not all.   *(put up cat)*

Raindrops, raindrops, where did they fall?
They fell on a blue bird, but that's not all.   *(put up bird)*

Raindrops, raindrops, where did they fall?
They fell on a yellow coat, but that's not all.   *(put up raincoat)*

Because up in the sky out came the sun,   *(put up sun)*
And the rain made a rainbow for everyone.   *(put up rainbow)*

ADDITIONAL ACTIVITY IDEAS

• The teacher takes the items off the board and asks the children to remember the color of each item.

• This poem can be used to study weather concepts as well as colors.

• The teacher can discuss colors that the children are wearing. The teacher sings "If You're Wearing Green, Please Stand Up," etc.

(5) Silly Clowns

(Put up pieces for the five clowns.)

Five silly clowns, jumping all around,
Jump so high, then touch the ground.
One silly clown said, "I can't stay,"
So she turned and hopped away.   *(take one clown off)*

Repeat with four, three, two, one, until no clowns are on the board; the teacher and the children then repeat the rhyme and act out the motions.

ADDITIONAL ACTIVITY IDEAS

• This poem can be used to illustrate math concepts as well as serve as a movement activity.

(5) Green Turtles

(Use blue yarn to make a circle for a lake; put up the pieces for the five turtles.)

Five green turtles swimming in the lake;
One crawled out with a stomach ache.   *(take off one turtle)*

Four green turtles swimming all together;
One crawled out to enjoy the sunny weather.   *(take off one turtle)*

Three green turtles swimming very fast;
One crawled out as her friends swam past.   *(take off one turtle)*

Two green turtles swimming on their way;
One crawled out to stop and play.   *(take off one turtle)*

One green turtle swimming all alone;
He crawled out to sit on a stone.   *(take off last turtle)*

The teacher repeats the rhyme and encourages the children to join him/her.

ADDITIONAL ACTIVITY IDEAS

• This poem can be used to illustrate math concepts.

Chicks and Bugs

(Put up five chicks.)

Five little chickens by the old barn door;   *(put up beetle)*
One chased a beetle and then there were four.   *(take off one chick and beetle)*

Four little chickens under a tree;   *(put up ant)*
One chased an ant and then there were three.   *(take off one chick and ant)*

Three little chickens looked for something new;   *(put up grasshopper)*
One saw a grasshopper—then there were two.   *(take off one chick and grasshopper)*

Two little chickens said, "Oh, what fun!"   *(put up ladybug)*
One saw a ladybug—then there was one.   *(take off one chick and ladybug)*

                                                   (put up bee)
One little chicken began to run;   *(take off last chick and bee)*
For he saw a bee—then there were none!

The teacher repeats the rhyme and encourages the children to join him/her.

ADDITIONAL ACTIVITY IDEAS

• The teacher puts all the insects on the flannel board. He/she then covers the board so the children can't see, removes one piece, and asks the children to guess which insect is missing.
• The insects can be used as part of a separate science lesson.
• Sing the song "I'm Bringing Home a Baby Bumble-Bee."

Clownfish

(Put up three little fish.)

Three little fish, swimming in a row;
Each one wondered how big they would grow.

The first fish thought, "What size will I be?"
She said, "Big would be just right for me."   *(exchange one little fish for big fish)*

The second fish thought, "What size will I be?"
He said, "Bigger would be OK for me."   *(exchange one little fish for bigger fish)*

The third fish wondered, "What size will I be?"
Then she said, "Biggest would be perfect for me!"   *(exchange last little fish for biggest fish)*

The teacher repeats the rhyme and encourages the children to join him/her.

ADDITIONAL ACTIVITY IDEAS

• The teacher can use other items that he/she has collected to teach the concept of comparative size. (Do not use the children—all children want to think they are big.)

Butterfly

One, two, three, four, five;   *(put up numerals 1-5)*
I caught a butterfly alive.   *(put up butterfly)*

Six, seven, eight, nine, ten;   *(put up numerals 6-10)*
I let him go again.   *(take off butterfly)*

The teacher and the children repeat the rhyme and act out the motions.

ADDITIONAL ACTIVITY IDEAS

• The teacher puts the numerals 1-10 on the board and the children count as he/she points to each one.

Big Bear, Little Bear

I'm Betty Bear and I'm five years old. I go to school and I can write my name. This is my little brother. He is just learning to talk.

(put up Betty Bear on right side of board)
(put Brother Bear on left side of board)

At night I sleep in a big bed, so I need a big pillow for my head. My brother sleeps in a crib so he uses a little pillow.

(put big pillow on right side)
(put little pillow on left side)

My hands are big so I need big gloves to stay warm. He's still small so he wears little mittens.

(put up gloves)
(put up mittens)

When we have breakfast, I drink my juice in a big glass, and he drinks his in a little cup.

(put up glass)
(put up cup)

I can dig a giant hole with my big shovel and my brother helps me with his little shovel.

(put up big shovel)
(put up little shovel)

I wear a big nightgown when I get dressed for bed. He wears little pajamas when he sleeps.

(put up nightgown)
(put up pajamas)

When we visit Grandma, I take my big doll and he takes his little bear.

(put up doll)
(put up little bear)

When I get hungry I eat a large ice cream cone and he licks a small one.

(put up large cone)
(put up small cone)

On my birthday I got a big present. It was a bicycle.

(put up bear on bicycle)

On my brother's birthday he got a small present. When he opened it, there was a little puppy.

(put up box)
(put up puppy)

Sometimes little can be fun!

ADDITIONAL ACTIVITY IDEAS

• The teacher shows a small box and a large box to the children. He/she then asks the children to guess what could be inside each, then opens the boxes and shows them a small and a large toy (equally interesting). The teacher asks each child if he/she prefers the large or small toy.

Friendly Shapes

Little Cindy Circle rolls along the ground;
She has no corners—she just spins around!   *(put up circle)*

Sammy Square is his name;
He has four sides, all the same . . . 1, 2, 3, 4!   *(put up square)*

Danny Diamond is shaped like a kite;
He has four points—I know that's right . . . 1, 2, 3, 4!   *(put up diamond)*

Tracy Triangle with corners three;
Count the corners now with me . . . 1, 2, 3!   *(put up triangle)*

ADDITIONAL RHYME

Make a circle, make a circle,   *(put up circle)*
Draw it in the sky.
Use your finger, use your finger,
Make it round as a pie.

Draw a square, draw a square,   *(put up square)*
Make the lines so straight.
Make a square, make a square,
Draw a box in the air.

Draw a triangle, draw a triangle,   *(put up triangle)*
Always start at the top.
Make a tent, make a tent,
Use three lines and stop!

ADDITIONAL ACTIVITY IDEAS

• The teacher holds up each shape and asks the children to name it.
• The teacher uses masking tape or yarn on the floor to make large shapes. The children can then take turns walking on them.
• The teacher gives each child an envelope with shapes. The teacher holds up a shape and asks the children to look in the envelopes for the matching shape.

Animal Shadows

Will you look and see,
Whose shadow this could be?

Put up each animal shadow one at a time—remove when children guess correctly.

ADDITIONAL RHYME

Elephant, elephant, what will you do?   *(put up elephant)*
Someone is standing in front of you.

Repeat with seal, penguin and rooster, putting each in front of the other. Then conclude with lion:

Lion, Lion, what will you do?   *(put up lion)*
No one is standing in front of you.
"I'll lead the parade, that's what I'll do!"

ADDITIONAL ACTIVITY IDEAS

• The teacher can line the animals up to be counted from left to right.
• The teacher can use the animals to teach concepts such as first/last, and middle/top/bottom/corner on the flannel board.

 # Little Mouse

(Put up all seven houses—hide mouse behind one house.)

Little mouse, little mouse;
Are you in the yellow house?   *(check behind the yellow house)*

Repeat for each color until the mouse is found under one of the houses.

ADDITIONAL ACTIVITY IDEAS

• The children can count the houses.
• The teacher can remove one house and have the children guess what color house is missing.

(8) # Balloons

Balloons, balloons, light as a feather,
Up in the air floating together.
We blew them all up and tied them so tight.
Let's name all the colors so pretty and bright.

(put up balloons as you say rhyme)

The children can name the colors from left to right.

ADDITIONAL ACTIVITY IDEAS

- The teacher can cut out various colored paper balloons and give each child his/her favorite color.
- Have a balloon race. The children can guess which will win. The teacher needs two different colored balloons. The children and the teacher sit in a circle. The teacher hands a balloon to each of the children sitting next to him/her. The children then pass the balloons around in opposite directions. The first one back to the teacher wins.

green

yellow raincoat

blue

yellow

23

purple

red

orange

"Raindrops"

light blue raindrops

gray

yellow
green
blue
purple
red

yellow sun

27

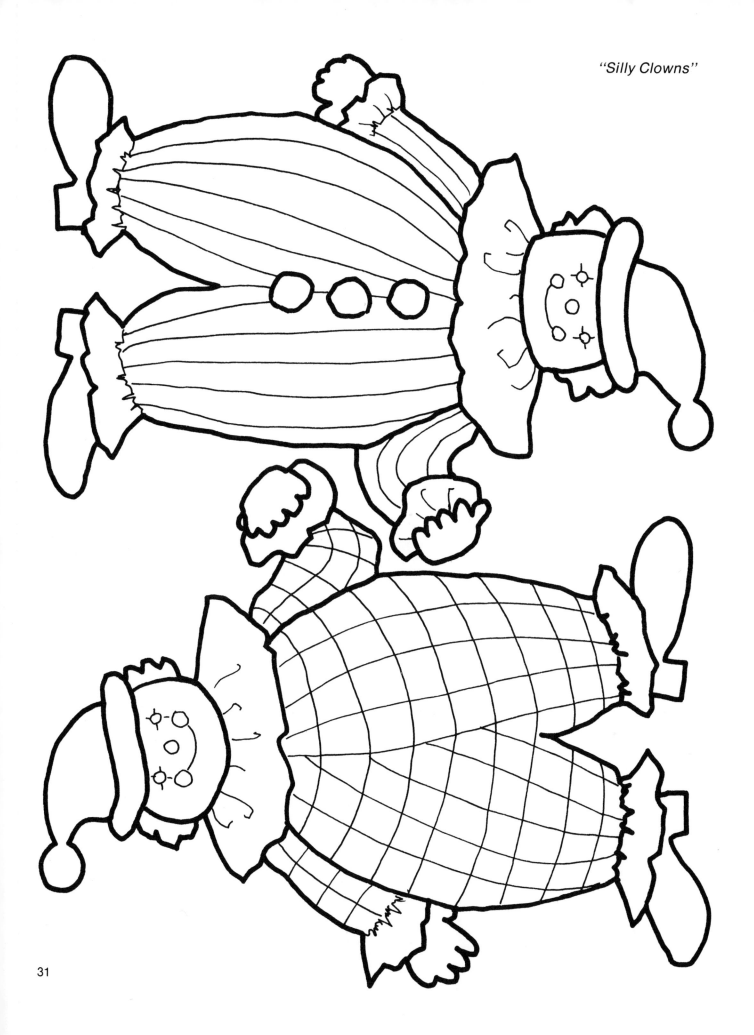

green turtles

33

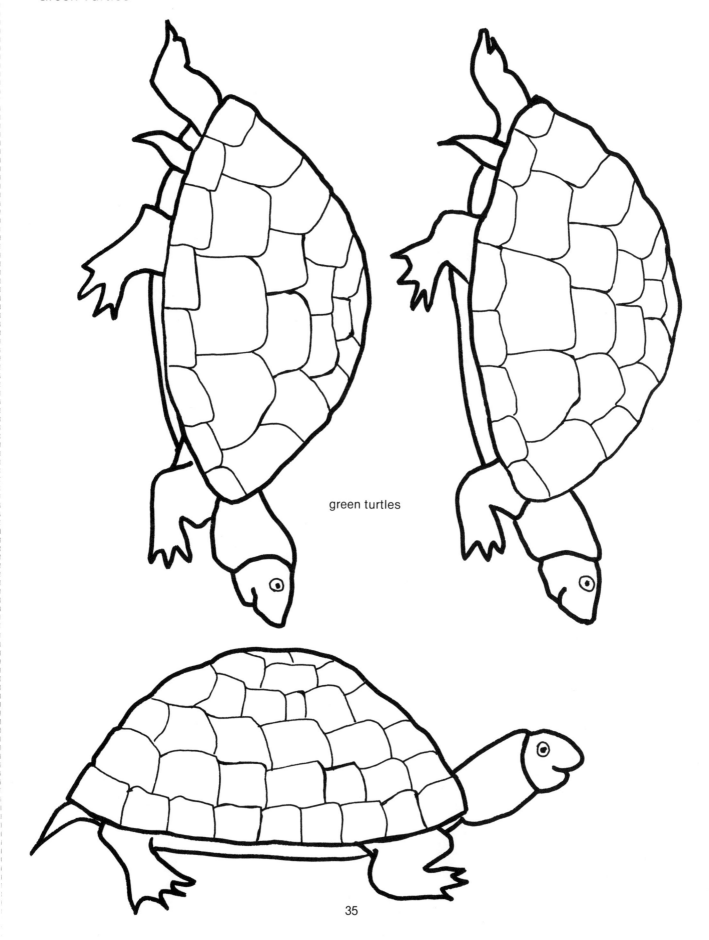

green turtles

35

"Chicks and Bugs"

yellow chicks, orange feet and beaks

light green
beetle

red
ladybug

green
grasshopper

yellow
bee

yellow chicks, orange feet and beaks

"Clownfish"

(big)

orange spots

(bigger)

orange

white

white

(color all six clownfish in this manner)

orange   white

41

pastel colors

(cut on line)

1 2 3 4 5
6 7 8 9 10

(biggest)

"Big Bear, Little Bear"

light brown bear

white pillows

yellow and blue suit

green stripes

yellow

pink gloves

red

light brown bear

green dress

45

"Big Bear, Little Bear"

black wheels

green dress

light brown bear

light brown

yellow

orange juice

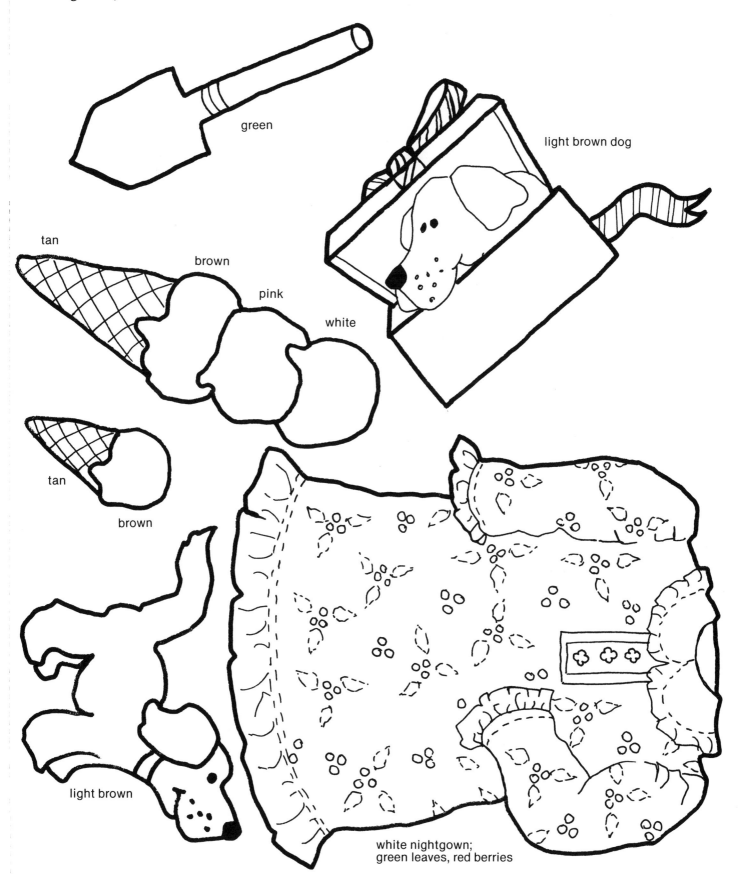

green

light brown dog

tan

brown

pink

white

tan

brown

light brown

white nightgown;
green leaves, red berries

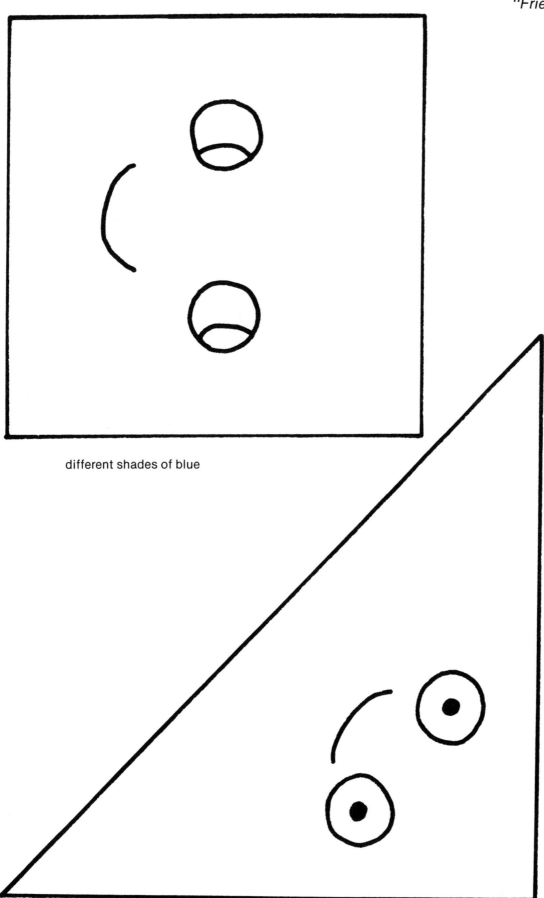

different shades of blue

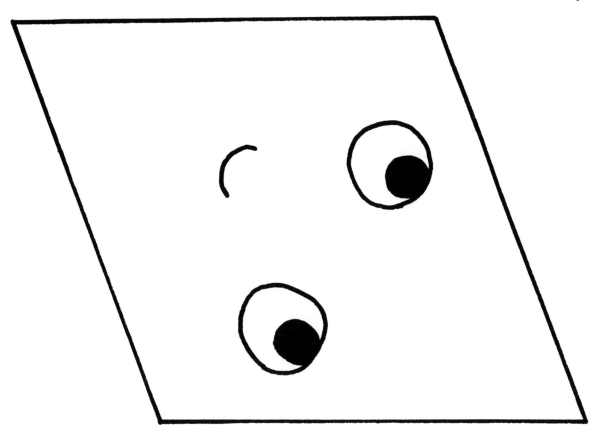

different shades of blue

59

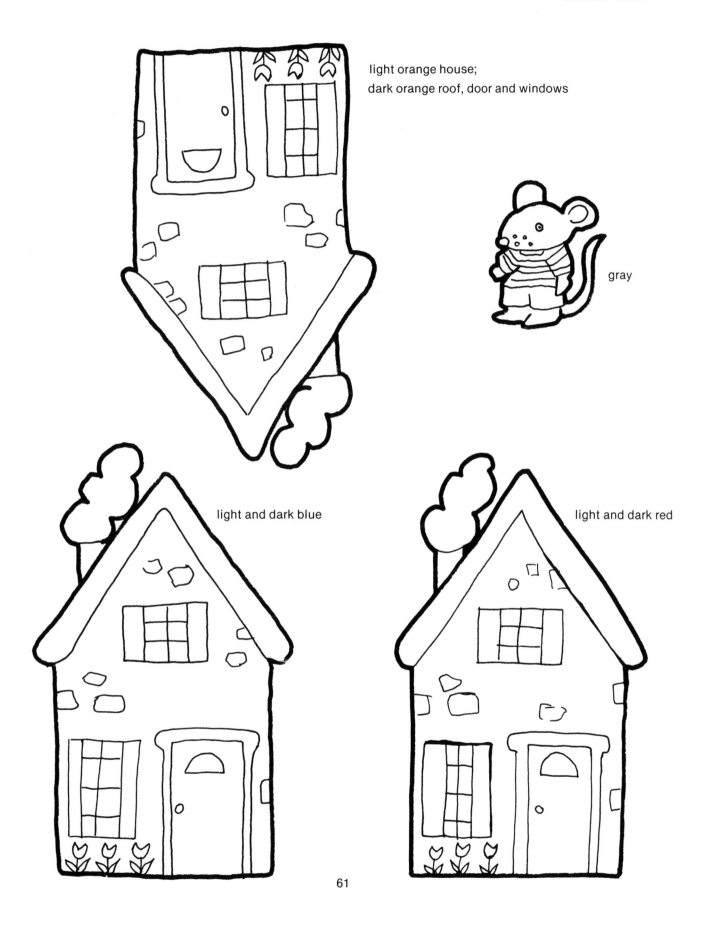

light orange house;
dark orange roof, door and windows

gray

light and dark blue

light and dark red

61

light and dark yellow

light and dark purple

light and dark green

light and dark pink

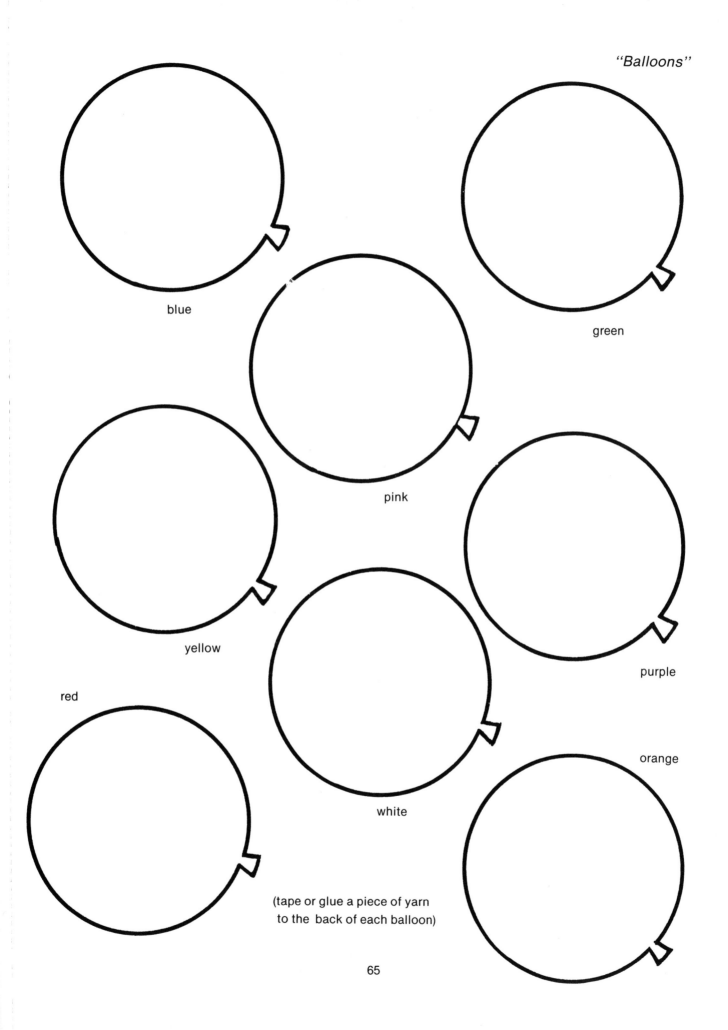

"Balloons"

blue

green

pink

yellow

purple

red

orange

white

(tape or glue a piece of yarn
to the back of each balloon)

65